PENGUIN BOOKS — GREAT IDEAS

Tao Te Ching

Lao Tzu

Tao Te Ching

TRANSLATED BY D. C. LAU

PENGUIN BOOKS — GREAT IDEAS

PENGUIN BOOKS

Published by the Penguin Group
Penguin Books Ltd, 80 Strand, London WC2R ORL, England
Penguin Group (USA) Inc., 375 Hudson Street, New York, New York 10014, USA
Penguin Group (Canada), 90 Eglinton Avenue East, Suite 700, Toronto, Ontario, Canada M4P 2Y3
(a division of Pearson Penguin Canada Inc.)
Penguin Ireland, 25 St Stephen's Green, Dublin 2, Ireland
(a division of Penguin Books Ltd)
Penguin Group (Australia), 250 Camberwell Road, Camberwell, Victoria 3124, Australia
(a division of Pearson Australia Group Pty Ltd)
Penguin Books India Pvt Ltd, 11 Community Centre, Panchsheel Park, New Delhi – 110 017, India
Penguin Group (NZ), 67 Apollo Drive, Rosedale, North Shore 0632, New Zealand
(a division of Pearson New Zealand Ltd)
Penguin Books (South Africa) (Pty) Ltd, 24 Sturdee Avenue,
Rosebank, Johannesburg 2196, South Africa

Penguin Books Ltd, Registered Offices: 80 Strand, London WC2R ORL, England

www.penguin.com

This translation first published 1963
This edition first published in Penguin Books 2009

010

Translation copyright © D. C. Lau, 1963
All rights reserved

The moral right of the translator has been asserted

Set by Rowland Phototypesetting Ltd, Bury St Edmunds, Suffolk
Printed in England by Clays Ltd, St Ives plc

978–0–141–04368–5

www.greenpenguin.co.uk

Book One

I

The way that can be spoken of
Is not the constant way;
The name that can be named
Is not the constant name.
The nameless was the beginning of heaven and earth;
The named was the mother of the myriad creatures.
Hence always rid yourself of desires in order to observe
    its secrets;
But always allow yourself to have desires in order to
    observe its manifestations.
These two are the same
But diverge in name as they issue forth.
Being the same they are called mysteries,
Mystery upon mystery –
The gateway of the manifold secrets.

II

The whole world recognizes the beautiful as the beautiful, yet this is only the ugly; the whole world recognizes the good as the good, yet this is only the bad.

Thus Something and Nothing produce each other;
The difficult and the easy complement each other;
The long and the short offset each other;
The high and the low incline towards each other;
Note and sound harmonize with each other;
Before and after follow each other.

Therefore the sage keeps to the deed that consists in taking no action and practises the teaching that uses no words.

The myriad creatures rise from it yet it claims no
authority;
It gives them life yet claims no possession;
It benefits them yet exacts no gratitude;
It accomplishes its task yet lays claim to no merit.

It is because it lays claim to no merit
That its merit never deserts it.

III

Not to honour men of worth will keep the people from contention; not to value goods which are hard to come by will keep them from theft; not to display what is desirable will keep them from being unsettled of mind.

Therefore in governing the people, the sage empties their minds but fills their bellies, weakens their wills but strengthens their bones. He always keeps them innocent of knowledge and free from desire, and ensures that the clever never dare to act.

Do that which consists in taking no action, and order will prevail.

IV

The way is empty, yet use will not drain it.
Deep, it is like the ancestor of the myriad creatures.
Blunt the sharpness;
Untangle the knots;
Soften the glare;
Let your wheels move only along old ruts.
Darkly visible, it only seems as if it were there.
I know not whose son it is.
It images the forefather of God.

V

Heaven and earth are ruthless, and treat the myriad creatures as straw dogs; the sage is ruthless, and treats the people as straw dogs.
Is not the space between heaven and earth like a bellows?
    It is empty without being exhausted:
    The more it works the more comes out.
    Much speech leads inevitably to silence.
    Better to hold fast to the void.

VI

The spirit of the valley never dies.
This is called the mysterious female.
The gateway of the mysterious female
Is called the root of heaven and earth.
Dimly visible, it seems as if it were there,
Yet use will never drain it.

VII

Heaven and earth are enduring. The reason why heaven and earth can be enduring is that they do not give themselves life. Hence they are able to be long-lived.

Therefore the sage puts his person last and it comes
        first,
Treats it as extraneous to himself and it is preserved.
Is it not because he is without thought of self that he is able to accomplish his private ends?

VIII

Highest good is like water. Because water excels in benefiting the myriad creatures without contending with them and settles where none would like to be, it comes close to the way.

In a home it is the site that matters;
In quality of mind it is depth that matters;
In an ally it is benevolence that matters;
In speech it is good faith that matters;
In government it is order that matters;
In affairs it is ability that matters;
In action it is timeliness that matters.

It is because it does not contend that it is never at fault.

IX

Rather than fill it to the brim by keeping it upright
Better to have stopped in time;
Hammer it to a point
And the sharpness cannot be preserved for ever;
There may be gold and jade to fill a hall
But there is none who can keep them.
To be overbearing when one has wealth and position
Is to bring calamity upon oneself.
To retire when the task is accomplished
Is the way of heaven.

X

When carrying on your head your perplexed bodily
    soul can you embrace in your arms the One
And not let go?
In concentrating your breath can you become as supple
As a babe?
Can you polish your mysterious mirror
And leave no blemish?
Can you love the people and govern the state
Without resorting to action?
When the gates of heaven open and shut
Are you capable of keeping to the role of the female?
When your discernment penetrates the four quarters
Are you capable of not knowing anything?
It gives them life and rears them.
It gives them life yet claims no possession;
It benefits them yet exacts no gratitude;
It is the steward yet exercises no authority.
Such is called the mysterious virtue.

XI

Thirty spokes
Share one hub.
Adapt the nothing therein to the purpose in hand, and you will have the use of the cart. Knead clay in order to make a vessel. Adapt the nothing therein to the purpose in hand, and you will have the use of the vessel. Cut out doors and windows in order to make a room. Adapt the nothing therein to the purpose in hand, and you will have the use of the room.

Thus what we gain is Something, yet it is by virtue of Nothing that this can be put to use.

XII

The five colours make man's eyes blind;
The five notes make his ears deaf;
The five tastes injure his palate;
Riding and hunting
Make his mind go wild with excitement;
Goods hard to come by
Serve to hinder his progress.
Hence the sage is
For the belly
Not for the eye.
Therefore he discards the one and takes the other.

XIII

Favour and disgrace are things that startle;
  High rank is, like one's body, a source of great
    trouble.
What is meant by saying that favour and disgrace are
things that startle? Favour when it is bestowed on a
subject serves to startle as much as when it is withdrawn.
This is what is meant by saying that favour and disgrace
are things that startle. What is meant by saying that high
rank is, like one's body, a source of great trouble? The
reason I have great trouble is that I have a body. When
I no longer have a body, what trouble have I?
Hence he who values his body more than dominion over
the empire can be entrusted with the empire. He who
loves his body more than dominion over the empire can
be given the custody of the empire.

XIV

What cannot be seen is called evanescent;
What cannot be heard is called rarefied;
What cannot be touched is called minute.
These three cannot be fathomed
And so they are confused and looked upon as one.
Its upper part is not dazzling;
Its lower part is not obscure.
Dimly visible, it cannot be named
And returns to that which is without substance.
This is called the shape that has no shape,
The image that is without substance.
This is called indistinct and shadowy.
Go up to it and you will not see its head;
Follow behind it and you will not see its rear.
Hold fast to the way of antiquity
In order to keep in control the realm of today.
The ability to know the beginning of antiquity
Is called the thread running through the way.

XV

Of old he who was well versed in the way
Was minutely subtle, mysteriously comprehending,
And too profound to be known.
It is because he could not be known
That he can only be given a makeshift description:
Tentative, as if fording a river in winter,
Hesitant, as if in fear of his neighbours;
Formal like a guest;
Falling apart like thawing ice;
Thick like the uncarved block;
Vacant like a valley;
Murky like muddy water.
Who can be muddy and yet, settling, slowly become
    limpid?
Who can be at rest and yet, stirring, slowly come to
    life?
He who holds fast to this way
Desires not to be full.
It is because he is not full
That he can be worn and yet newly made.

XVI

I do my utmost to attain emptiness;
I hold firmly to stillness.
The myriad creatures all rise together
And I watch their return.
The teeming creatures
All return to their separate roots.
Returning to one's roots is known as stillness.
This is what is meant by returning to one's destiny.
Returning to one's destiny is known as the constant.
Knowledge of the constant is known as discernment.
Woe to him who wilfully innovates
While ignorant of the constant,
But should one act from knowledge of the constant
One's action will lead to impartiality,
Impartiality to kingliness,
Kingliness to heaven,
Heaven to the way,
The way to perpetuity,
And to the end of one's days one will meet with no
    danger.

XVII

The best of all rulers is but a shadowy presence to his
subjects.
    Next comes the ruler they love and praise;
    Next comes one they fear;
    Next comes one with whom they take liberties.
When there is not enough faith, there is lack of good
      faith.
    Hesitant, he does not utter words lightly.
    When his task is accomplished and his work done
    The people all say, 'It happened to us naturally.'

XVIII

When the great way falls into disuse
There are benevolence and rectitude;
When cleverness emerges
There is great hypocrisy;
When the six relations are at variance
There are filial children;
When the state is benighted
There are loyal ministers.

XIX

Exterminate the sage, discard the wise,
And the people will benefit a hundredfold;
Exterminate benevolence, discard rectitude,
And the people will again be filial;
Exterminate ingenuity, discard profit,
And there will be no more thieves and bandits.
These three, being false adornments, are not enough
And the people must have something to which they
    can attach themselves:
Exhibit the unadorned and embrace the uncarved
    block,
Have little thought of self and as few desires as
    possible.

XX

Exterminate learning and there will no longer be
    worries.
Between yea and nay
How much difference is there?
Between good and evil
How great is the distance?
What others fear
One must also fear.
And wax without having reached the limit.
The multitude are joyous
As if partaking of the *t'ai lao* offering
Or going up to a terrace in spring.
I alone am inactive and reveal no signs,
Like a baby that has not yet learned to smile,
Listless as though with no home to go back to.
The multitude all have more than enough.
I alone seem to be in want.
My mind is that of a fool – how blank!
Vulgar people are clear.
I alone am drowsy.
Vulgar people are alert.
I alone am muddled.
Calm like the sea;
Like a high wind that never ceases.
The multitude all have a purpose.
I alone am foolish and uncouth.
I alone am different from others
And value being fed by the mother.

XXI

In his every movement a man of great virtue
Follows the way and the way only.
As a thing the way is
Shadowy, indistinct.
Indistinct and shadowy,
Yet within it is an image;
Shadowy and indistinct,
Yet within it is a substance.
Dim and dark,
Yet within it is an essence.
This essence is quite genuine
And within it is something that can be tested.
From the present back to antiquity
Its name never deserted it.
It serves as a means for inspecting the fathers of the
    multitude.
How do I know that the fathers of the multitude are like
that? By means of this.

XXII

Bowed down then preserved;
Bent then straight;
Hollow then full;
Worn then new;
A little then benefited;
A lot then perplexed.
Therefore the sage embraces the One and is a model
    for the empire.
He does not show himself, and so is conspicuous;
He does not consider himself right, and so is
    illustrious;
He does not brag, and so has merit;
He does not boast, and so endures.
It is because he does not contend that no one in the
empire is in a position to contend with him.
The way the ancients had it, 'Bowed down then pre-
served', is no empty saying. Truly it enables one to be
preserved to the end.

XXIII

To use words but rarely
   Is to be natural.
Hence a gusty wind cannot last all morning, and a sudden
downpour cannot last all day. Who is it that produces
these? Heaven and earth. If even heaven and earth cannot
go on for ever, much less can man. That is why one
follows the way.

A man of the way conforms to the way; a man of virtue
conforms to virtue; a man of loss conforms to loss. He
who conforms to the way is gladly accepted by the way;
he who conforms to virtue is gladly accepted by virtue;
he who conforms to loss is gladly accepted by loss.

When there is not enough faith, there is lack of good
faith.

XXIV

He who tiptoes cannot stand; he who strides cannot
     walk.
   He who shows himself is not conspicuous;
   He who considers himself right is not illustrious;
   He who brags will have no merit;
   He who boasts will not endure.
From the point of view of the way these are 'excessive
food and useless excrescences'. As there are Things that
detest them, he who has the way does not abide in them.

XXV

There is a thing confusedly formed,
Born before heaven and earth.
Silent and void
It stands alone and does not change,
Goes round and does not weary.
It is capable of being the mother of the world.
I know not its name
So I style it 'the way'.
I give it the makeshift name of 'the great'.
Being great, it is further described as receding,
Receding, it is described as far away,
Being far away, it is described as turning back.
Hence the way is great; heaven is great; earth is great;
and the king is also great. Within the realm there are
four things that are great, and the king counts as one.
Man models himself on earth,
Earth on heaven,
Heaven on the way,
And the way on that which is naturally so.

XXVI

The heavy is the root of the light;
The still is the lord of the restless.
Therefore the gentleman when travelling all day
Never lets the heavily laden carts out of his sight.
It is only when he is safely behind walls and
    watchtowers
That he rests peacefully and is above worries.
How, then, should a ruler of ten thousand chariots
Make light of his own person in the eyes of the empire?
If light, then the root is lost;
If restless, then the lord is lost.

XXVII

One who excels in travelling leaves no wheel tracks;
One who excels in speech makes no slips;
One who excels in reckoning uses no counting rods;
One who excels in shutting uses no bolts yet what
    he has shut cannot be opened;
One who excels in tying uses no cords yet what he
    has tied cannot be undone.
Therefore the sage always excels in saving people, and
so abandons no one; always excels in saving things, and
so abandons nothing.
This is called following one's discernment.
    Hence the good man is the teacher the bad learns
      from;
    And the bad man is the material the good works on.
    Not to value the teacher
    Nor to love the material
    Though it seems clever, betrays great bewilderment.
This is called the essential and the secret.

XXVIII

Know the male
But keep to the role of the female
And be a ravine to the empire.
If you are a ravine to the empire,
Then the constant virtue will not desert you
And you will again return to being a babe.
Know the white
But keep to the role of the black
And be a model to the empire.
If you are a model to the empire,
Then the constant virtue will not be wanting
And you will return to the infinite.
Know honour
But keep to the role of the disgraced
And be a valley to the empire.
If you are a valley to the empire,
Then the constant virtue will be sufficient
And you will return to being the uncarved block.
When the uncarved block shatters it becomes vessels.
The sage makes use of these and becomes the lord over
the officials.
Hence the greatest cutting
Does not sever.

XXIX

Whoever takes the empire and wishes to do anything to it I see will have no respite. The empire is a sacred vessel and nothing should be done to it. Whoever does anything to it will ruin it; whoever lays hold of it will lose it.

Hence some things lead and some follow;
Some breathe gently and some breathe hard;
Some are strong and some are weak;
Some destroy and some are destroyed.

Therefore the sage avoids excess, extravagance, and arrogance.

XXX

One who assists the ruler of men by means of the way
does not intimidate the empire by a show of arms.

This is something which is liable to rebound.

Where troops have encamped

There will brambles grow;

In the wake of a mighty army

Bad harvests follow without fail.

One who is good aims only at bringing his campaign to
a conclusion and dare not thereby intimidate. Bring it to
a conclusion but do not boast; bring it to a conclusion
but do not brag; bring it to a conclusion but do not be
arrogant; bring it to a conclusion but only when there is
no choice; bring it to a conclusion but do not intimidate.

A creature in its prime doing harm to the old

Is known as going against the way.

That which goes against the way will come to an
early end.

XXXI

It is because arms are instruments of ill omen and there are Things that detest them that one who has the way does not abide by their use. The gentleman gives precedence to the left when at home, but to the right when he goes to war. Arms are instruments of ill omen, not the instruments of the gentleman. When one is compelled to use them, it is best to do so without relish. There is no glory in victory, and to glorify it despite this is to exult in the killing of men. One who exults in the killing of men will never have his way in the empire. On occasions of rejoicing precedence is given to the left; on occasions of mourning precedence is given to the right. A lieutenant's place is on the left; the general's place is on the right. This means that it is mourning rites that are observed. When great numbers of people are killed, one should weep over them with sorrow. When victorious in war, one should observe the rites of mourning.

XXXII

The way is for ever nameless.
Though the uncarved block is small
No one in the world dare claim its allegiance.
Should lords and princes be able to hold fast to it
The myriad creatures will submit of their own
    accord,
Heaven and earth will unite and sweet dew will fall,
And the people will be equitable, though no one so
    decrees.
Only when it is cut are there names.
As soon as there are names
One ought to know that it is time to stop.
Knowing when to stop one can be free from danger.
The way is to the world as the River and the Sea are to
rivulets and streams.

XXXIII

He who knows others is clever;
He who knows himself has discernment.
He who overcomes others has force;
He who overcomes himself is strong.
He who knows contentment is rich;
He who perseveres is a man of purpose;
He who does not lose his station will endure;
He who lives out his days has had a long life.

XXXIV

The way is broad, reaching left as well as right.
The myriad creatures depend on it for life yet it
claims no authority.
It accomplishes its task yet lays claim to no merit.
It clothes and feeds the myriad creatures yet lays no
claim to being their master.
For ever free of desire, it can be called small; yet, as it
lays no claim to being master when the myriad creatures
turn to it, it can be called great.
It is because it never attempts itself to be great that it
succeeds in becoming great.

XXXV

Have in your hold the great image
And the empire will come to you.
Coming to you and meeting with no harm
It will be safe and sound.
Music and food
Will induce the wayfarer to stop.
The way in its passage through the mouth is
     without flavour.
It cannot be seen,
It cannot be heard,
Yet it cannot be exhausted by use.

XXXVI

If you would have a thing shrink,
You must first stretch it;
If you would have a thing weakened,
You must first strengthen it;
If you would have a thing laid aside,
You must first set it up;
If you would take from a thing,
You must first give to it.
This is called subtle discernment:
The submissive and weak will overcome the hard and
    strong.
The fish must not be allowed to leave the deep;
The instruments of power in a state must not be
    revealed to anyone.

XXXVII

The way never acts yet nothing is left undone.
Should lords and princes be able to hold fast to it,
The myriad creatures will be transformed of their own
    accord.
After they are transformed, should desire raise its head,
I shall press it down with the weight of the nameless
    uncarved block.
The nameless uncarved block
Is but freedom from desire,
And if I cease to desire and remain still,
The empire will be at peace of its own accord.

Book Two

XXXVIII

A man of the highest virtue does not keep to virtue and that is why he has virtue. A man of the lowest virtue never strays from virtue and that is why he is without virtue. The former never acts yet leaves nothing undone. The latter acts but there are things left undone. A man of the highest benevolence acts, but from no ulterior motive. A man of the highest rectitude acts, but from ulterior motive. A man most conversant in the rites acts, but when no one responds rolls up his sleeves and resorts to persuasion by force.

Hence when the way was lost there was virtue; when virtue was lost there was benevolence; when benevolence was lost there was rectitude; when rectitude was lost there were the rites.

The rites are the wearing thin of loyalty and good
    faith
And the beginning of disorder;
Foreknowledge is the flowery embellishment of the
    way
And the beginning of folly.

Hence the man of large mind abides in the thick not in the thin, in the fruit not in the flower.

Therefore he discards the one and takes the other.

XXXIX

Of old, these came to be in possession of the One:
  Heaven in virtue of the One is limpid;
  Earth in virtue of the One is settled;
  Gods in virtue of the One have their potencies;
  The valley in virtue of the One is full;
  The myriad creatures in virtue of the One are alive;
  Lords and princes in virtue of the One become
      leaders in the empire.
It is the One that makes these what they are.
  Without what makes it limpid heaven might split;
  Without what makes it settled earth might sink;
  Without what gives them their potencies gods might
      spend themselves;
  Without what makes it full the valley might run dry;
  Without what keeps them alive the myriad creatures
      might perish;
  Without what makes them leaders lords and princes
      might fall.
Hence the superior must have the inferior as root; the
high must have the low as base.
Thus lords and princes refer to themselves as 'solitary',
'desolate', and 'hapless'. This is taking the inferior as
root, is it not?
  Hence the highest renown is without renown,
  Not wishing to be one among many like jade
  Nor to be aloof like stone.

XL

Turning back is how the way moves;
Weakness is the means the way employs.
The myriad creatures in the world are born from Something, and Something from Nothing.

XLI

When the best student hears about the way
He practises it assiduously;
When the average student hears about the way
It seems to him one moment there and gone the
    next;
When the worst student hears about the way
He laughs out loud.
If he did not laugh
It would be unworthy of being the way.
Hence the *Chien yen* has it:
The way that is bright seems dull;
The way that leads forward seems to lead backward;
The way that is even seems rough.
The highest virtue is like the valley;
The sheerest whiteness seems sullied;
Ample virtue seems defective;
Vigorous virtue seems indolent;
Plain virtue seems soiled;
The great square has no corners.
The great vessel takes long to complete;
The great note is rarefied in sound;
The great image has no shape.
The way conceals itself in being nameless.
It is the way alone that excels in bestowing and in
    accomplishing.

XLII

The way begets one; one begets two; two begets three; three begets the myriad creatures.

The myriad creatures carry on their backs the *yin* and embrace in their arms the *yang* and are the blending of the generative forces of the two.

There are no words which men detest more than 'solitary', 'desolate', and 'hapless', yet lords and princes use these to refer to themselves.

Thus a thing is sometimes added to by being diminished and diminished by being added to.

What others teach I also teach. 'The violent will not come to a natural end.' I shall take this as my precept.

XLIII

The most submissive thing in the world can ride rough-shod over the hardest in the world – that which is without substance entering that which has no crevices. That is why I know the benefit of resorting to no action. The teaching that uses no words, the benefit of resorting to no action, these are beyond the understanding of all but a very few in the world.

XLIV

Your name or your person,
Which is dearer?
Your person or your goods,
Which is worth more?
Gain or loss,
Which is a greater bane?
That is why excessive meanness
Is sure to lead to great expense;
Too much store
Is sure to end in immense loss.
Know contentment
And you will suffer no disgrace;
Know when to stop
And you will meet with no danger.
You can then endure.

XLV

Great perfection seems chipped,
Yet use will not wear it out;
Great fullness seems empty,
Yet use will not drain it;
Great straightness seems bent;
Great skill seems awkward;
Great eloquence seems tongue-tied.
Restlessness overcomes cold; stillness overcomes heat.
Limpid and still,
One can be a leader in the empire.

XLVI

When the way prevails in the empire, fleet-footed horses are relegated to ploughing the fields; when the way does not prevail in the empire, war-horses breed on the border.

There is no crime greater than having too many
  desires;
There is no disaster greater than not being content;
There is no misfortune greater than being covetous.
Hence in being content, one will always have enough.

XLVII

Without stirring abroad
One can know the whole world;
Without looking out of the window
One can see the way of heaven.
The further one goes
The less one knows.
Therefore the sage knows without having to stir,
Identifies without having to see,
Accomplishes without having to act.

XLVIII

In the pursuit of learning one knows more every day; in the pursuit of the way one does less every day. One does less and less until one does nothing at all, and when one does nothing at all there is nothing that is undone.

It is always through not meddling that the empire is won. Should you meddle, then you are not equal to the task of winning the empire.

XLIX

The sage has no mind of his own. He takes as his own the mind of the people.

Those who are good I treat as good. Those who are not good I also treat as good. In so doing I gain in goodness. Those who are of good faith I have faith in. Those who are lacking in good faith I also have faith in. In so doing I gain in good faith.

The sage in his attempt to distract the mind of the empire seeks urgently to muddle it. The people all have something to occupy their eyes and ears, and the sage treats them all like children.

L

When going one way means life and going the other means death, three in ten will be comrades of life, three in ten will be comrades of death, and there are those who value life and as a result move into the realm of death, and these also number three in ten. Why is this so? Because they set too much store by life. I have heard it said that one who excels in safeguarding his own life does not meet with rhinoceros or tiger when travelling on land nor is he touched by weapons when charging into an army. There is nowhere for the rhinoceros to pitch its horn; there is nowhere for the tiger to place its claws; there is nowhere for the weapon to lodge its blade. Why is this so? Because for him there is no realm of death.

LI

The way gives them life;
Virtue rears them;
Things give them shape;
Circumstances bring them to maturity.
Therefore the myriad creatures all revere the way and
honour virtue. Yet the way is revered and virtue honoured
not because this is decreed by any authority but because
it is natural for them to be treated so.
Thus the way gives them life and rears them;
Brings them up and nurses them;
Brings them to fruition and maturity;
Feeds and shelters them.
It gives them life yet claims no possession;
It benefits them yet exacts no gratitude;
It is the steward yet exercises no authority.
Such is called the mysterious virtue.

LII

The world had a beginning
And this beginning could be the mother of the world.
When you know the mother
Go on to know the child.
After you have known the child
Go back to holding fast to the mother,
And to the end of your days you will not meet with
     danger.
Block the openings,
Shut the doors,
And all your life you will not run dry.
Unblock the openings,
Add to your troubles,
And to the end of your days you will be beyond
     salvation.
To see the small is called discernment;
To hold fast to the submissive is called strength.
Use the light
But give up the discernment.
Bring not misfortune upon yourself.
This is known as following the constant.

LIII

Were I possessed of the least knowledge, I would, when
walking on the great way, fear only paths that lead astray.
The great way is easy, yet people prefer by-paths.

    The court is corrupt,
    The fields are overgrown with weeds,
    The granaries are empty;
    Yet there are those dressed in fineries,
    With swords at their sides,
    Filled with food and drink,
    And possessed of too much wealth.
    This is known as taking the lead in robbery.
Far indeed is this from the way.

LIV

What is firmly rooted cannot be pulled out;
What is tightly held in the arms will not slip loose;
Through this the offering of sacrifice by descendants
    will never come to an end.
Cultivate it in your person
And its virtue will be genuine;
Cultivate it in the family
And its virtue will be more than sufficient;
Cultivate it in the hamlet
And its virtue will endure;
Cultivate it in the state
And its virtue will abound;
Cultivate it in the empire
And its virtue will be pervasive.
Hence look at the person through the person; look at the family through the family; look at the hamlet through the hamlet; look at the state through the state; look at the empire through the empire.
How do I know that the empire is like that? By means of this.

LV

One who possesses virtue in abundance is comparable
to a new born babe:
    Poisonous insects will not sting it;
    Ferocious animals will not pounce on it;
    Predatory birds will not swoop down on it.
    Its bones are weak and its sinews supple yet its hold
        is firm.
    It does not know of the union of male and female
        yet its male member will stir:
This is because its virility is at its height.
    It howls all day yet does not become hoarse:
This is because its harmony is at its height.
    To know harmony is called the constant;
    To know the constant is called discernment.
    To try to add to one's vitality is called ill-omened;
    For the mind to egg on the breath is called violent.
    A creature in its prime doing harm to the old
    Is known as going against the way.
    That which goes against the way will come to an
        early end.

LVI

One who knows does not speak; one who speaks does not know.

    Block the openings;
    Shut the doors.
    Blunt the sharpness;
    Untangle the knots;
    Soften the glare;
    Let your wheels move only along old ruts.

This is known as mysterious sameness.

Hence you cannot get close to it, nor can you keep it at arm's length; you cannot bestow benefit on it, nor can you do it harm; you cannot ennoble it, nor can you debase it.

Therefore it is valued by the empire.

LVII

Govern the state by being straightforward; wage war by being crafty; but win the empire by not being meddlesome.

How do I know that it is like that? By means of this.

The more taboos there are in the empire

The poorer the people;

The more sharpened tools the people have

The more benighted the state;

The more skills the people have

The further novelties multiply;

The better known the laws and edicts

The more thieves and robbers there are.

Hence the sage says,

I take no action and the people are transformed of
themselves;

I prefer stillness and the people are rectified of
themselves;

I am not meddlesome and the people prosper of
themselves;

I am free from desire and the people of themselves
become simple like the uncarved block.

LVIII

When the government is muddled
The people are simple;
When the government is alert
The people are cunning.
It is on disaster that good fortune perches;
It is beneath good fortune that disaster crouches.
Who knows the limit? Does not the straightforward
exist?
The straightforward changes again into the crafty, and
the good changes again into the monstrous. Indeed, it is
long since the people were perplexed.

Therefore the sage is square-edged but does not
   scrape,
Has corners but does not jab,
Extends himself but not at the expense of others,
Shines but does not dazzle.

LIX

In ruling the people and in serving heaven it is best for
    a ruler to be sparing.
It is because he is sparing
That he may be said to follow the way from the start;
Following the way from the start he may be said to
    accumulate an abundance of virtue;
Accumulating an abundance of virtue there is nothing
    he cannot overcome;
When there is nothing he cannot overcome, no one
    knows his limit;
When no one knows his limit
He can possess a state;
When he possesses the mother of a state
He can then endure.
This is called the way of deep roots and firm stems by
    which one lives to see many days.

LX

Governing a large state is like boiling a small fish.
When the empire is ruled in accordance with the way,
   The spirits lose their potencies.
   Or rather, it is not that they lose their potencies,
   But that, though they have their potencies, they do
      not harm the people.
   It is not only they who, having their potencies, do
      not harm the people,
   The sage, also, does not harm the people.
As neither does any harm, each attributes the merit to
the other.

LXI

A large state is the lower reaches of a river –
The place where all the streams of the world unite.
In the union of the world,
The female always gets the better of the male by
    stillness.
Being still, she takes the lower position.
Hence the large state, by taking the lower position,
    annexes the small state;
The small state, by taking the lower position,
    affiliates itself to the large state.
Thus the one, by taking the lower position, annexes;
The other, by taking the lower position, is annexed.
All that the large state wants is to take the other
    under its wing;
All that the small state wants is to have its services
    accepted by the other.
If each of the two wants to find its proper place,
It is meet that the large should take the lower
    position.

LXII

The way is the refuge for the myriad creatures.
It is that by which the good man protects,
And that by which the bad is protected.
Beautiful words when offered will win high rank in
    return;
Beautiful deeds can raise a man above others.
Even if a man is not good, why should he be abandoned?
Hence when the emperor is set up and the three ducal
ministers are appointed, he who makes a present of the
way without stirring from his seat is preferable to one
who offers presents of jade disks followed by a team of
four horses. Why was this way valued of old? Was it not
said that by means of it one got what one wanted and
escaped the consequences when one transgressed?
Therefore it is valued by the empire.

LXIII

Do that which consists in taking no action; pursue that which is not meddlesome; savour that which has no flavour.

Make the small big and the few many; do good to him who has done you an injury.

Lay plans for the accomplishment of the difficult before it becomes difficult; make something big by starting with it when small.

Difficult things in the world must needs have their beginnings in the easy; big things must needs have their beginnings in the small.

Therefore it is because the sage never attempts to be great that he succeeds in becoming great.

One who makes promises rashly rarely keeps good faith; one who is in the habit of considering things easy meets with frequent difficulties.

Therefore even the sage treats some things as difficult. That is why in the end no difficulties can get the better of him.

LXIV

It is easy to maintain a situation while it is still secure;
It is easy to deal with a situation before symptoms
    develop;
It is easy to break a thing when it is yet brittle;
It is easy to dissolve a thing when it is yet minute.
Deal with a thing while it is still nothing;
Keep a thing in order before disorder sets in.
A tree that can fill the span of a man's arms
Grows from a downy tip;
A terrace nine storeys high
Rises from hodfuls of earth;
A journey of a thousand miles
Starts from beneath one's feet.

Whoever does anything to it will ruin it; whoever lays
hold of it will lose it.

Therefore the sage, because he does nothing, never ruins
anything; and, because he does not lay hold of anything,
loses nothing.

In their enterprises the people
Always ruin them when on the verge of success.
Be as careful at the end as at the beginning
And there will be no ruined enterprises.
Therefore the sage desires not to desire
And does not value goods which are hard to come by;
Learns to be without learning
And makes good the mistakes of the multitude
In order to help the myriad creatures to be natural
    and to refrain from daring to act.

LXV

Of old those who excelled in the pursuit of the way did not use it to enlighten the people but to hoodwink them. The reason why the people are difficult to govern is that they are too clever.

Hence to rule a state by cleverness
Will be to the detriment of the state;
Not to rule a state by cleverness
Will be a boon to the state.
These two are models.
Always to know the models
Is known as mysterious virtue.
Mysterious virtue is profound and far-reaching,
But when things turn back it turns back with them.
Only then is complete conformity realized.

LXVI

The reason why the River and the Sea are able to be king of the hundred valleys is that they excel in taking the lower position. Hence they are able to be king of the hundred valleys.

Therefore, desiring to rule over the people,
One must in one's words humble oneself before
    them;
And, desiring to lead the people,
One must, in one's person, follow behind them.
Therefore the sage takes his place over the people yet is no burden; takes his place ahead of the people yet causes no obstruction. That is why the empire supports him joyfully and never tires of doing so.
It is because he does not contend that no one in the empire is in a position to contend with him.

LXVII

The whole world says that my way is vast and resembles nothing. It is because it is vast that it resembles nothing. If it resembled anything, it would, long before now, have become small.

I have three treasures
Which I hold and cherish.
The first is known as compassion,
The second is known as frugality,
The third is known as not daring to take the lead in
the empire;
Being compassionate one could afford to be
courageous,
Being frugal one could afford to extend one's
territory,
Not daring to take the lead in the empire one could
afford to be lord over the vessels.

Now, to forsake compassion for courage, to forsake frugality for expansion, to forsake the rear for the lead, is sure to end in death.

Through compassion, one will triumph in attack and be impregnable in defence. What heaven succours it protects with the gift of compassion.

LXVIII

One who excels as a warrior does not appear
    formidable;
One who excels in fighting is never roused in anger;
One who excels in defeating his enemy does not join
    issue;
One who excels in employing others humbles himself
    before them.
This is known as the virtue of non-contention;
This is known as making use of the efforts of others;
This is known as matching the sublimity of heaven.

LXIX

The strategists have a saying,
I dare not play the host but play the guest,
I dare not advance an inch but retreat a foot instead.
This is known as marching forward when there is no
     road,
Rolling up one's sleeves when there is no arm,
Dragging one's adversary by force when there is no
     adversary,
And taking up arms when there are no arms.
There is no disaster greater than taking on an enemy too
easily. So doing nearly cost me my treasure. Thus of two
sides raising arms against each other, it is the one that is
sorrow-stricken that wins.

LXX

My words are very easy to understand and very easy to put into practice, yet no one in the world can understand them or put them into practice.
Words have an ancestor and affairs have a sovereign.
It is because people are ignorant that they fail to understand me.

Those who understand me are few;
Those who imitate me are honoured.

Therefore the sage, while clad in homespun, conceals on his person a priceless piece of jade.

LXXI

To know yet to think that one does not know is best;
  Not to know yet to think that one knows will lead to
    difficulty.
It is by being alive to difficulty that one can avoid it. The
sage meets with no difficulty. It is because he is alive to
it that he meets with no difficulty.

LXXII

When the people lack a proper sense of awe, then some awful visitation will descend upon them.

Do not constrict their living space; do not press down on their means of livelihood. It is because you do not press down on them that they will not weary of the burden.

Hence the sage knows himself but does not display himself, loves himself but does not exalt himself.

Therefore he discards the one and takes the other.

LXXIII

He who is fearless in being bold will meet with his
      death;
He who is fearless in being timid will stay alive.
Of the two, one leads to good, the other to harm.
Heaven hates what it hates,
Who knows the reason why?
Therefore even the sage treats some things as difficult.
The way of heaven
    Excels in overcoming though it does not contend,
    In responding though it does not speak,
    In attracting though it does not summon,
    In laying plans though it appears slack.
The net of heaven is cast wide. Though the mesh is not
fine, yet nothing ever slips through.

LXXIV

When the people are not afraid of death, wherefore frighten them with death? Were the people always afraid of death, and were I able to arrest and put to death those who innovate, then who would dare? There is a regular executioner whose charge it is to kill. To kill on behalf of the executioner is what is described as chopping wood on behalf of the master carpenter. In chopping wood on behalf of the master carpenter, there are few who escape hurting their own hands instead.

LXXV

The people are hungry:
It is because those in authority eat up too much in
    taxes
That the people are hungry.
The people are difficult to govern:
It is because those in authority are too fond of action
That the people are difficult to govern.
The people treat death lightly:
It is because the people set too much store by life
That they treat death lightly.
It is just because one has no use for life that one is wiser
than the man who values life.

LXXVI

A man is supple and weak when living, but hard and stiff when dead. Grass and trees are pliant and fragile when living, but dried and shrivelled when dead. Thus the hard and the strong are the comrades of death; the supple and the weak are the comrades of life.

Therefore a weapon that is strong will not vanquish;
A tree that is strong will suffer the axe.
The strong and big takes the lower position,
The supple and weak takes the higher position.

LXXVII

Is not the way of heaven like the stretching of a bow?
   The high it presses down,
   The low it lifts up;
   The excessive it takes from,
   The deficient it gives to.
It is the way of heaven to take from what has in excess
in order to make good what is deficient. The way of man
is otherwise. It takes from those who are in want in
order to offer this to those who already have more than
enough. Who is there that can take what he himself has
in excess and offer this to the empire? Only he who has
the way.
   Therefore the sage benefits them yet exacts no
      gratitude,
   Accomplishes his task yet lays claim to no merit.
Is this not because he does not wish to be considered a
better man than others?

LXXVIII

In the world there is nothing more submissive and weak than water. Yet for attacking that which is hard and strong nothing can surpass it. This is because there is nothing that can take its place.

That the weak overcomes the strong,
And the submissive overcomes the hard,
Everyone in the world knows yet no one can put
    this knowledge into practice.
Therefore the sage says,
One who takes on himself the humiliation of the
    state
Is called a ruler worthy of offering sacrifices to the
    gods of earth and millet;
One who takes on himself the calamity of the state
Is called a king worthy of dominion over the entire
    empire.
Straightforward words
Seem paradoxical.

LXXIX

When peace is made between great enemies,
Some enmity is bound to remain undispelled.
How can this be considered perfect?
Therefore the sage takes the left-hand tally, but exacts
no payment from the people.
The man of virtue takes charge of the tally;
The man of no virtue takes charge of exaction.
It is the way of heaven to show no favouritism.
It is for ever on the side of the good man.

LXXX

Reduce the size and population of the state. Ensure that even though the people have tools of war for a troop or a battalion they will not use them; and also that they will be reluctant to move to distant places because they look on death as no light matter.

Even when they have ships and carts, they will have no use for them; and even when they have armour and weapons, they will have no occasion to make a show of them.

Bring it about that the people will return to the use of the knotted rope,

Will find relish in their food
And beauty in their clothes,
Will be content in their abode
And happy in the way they live.

Though adjoining states are within sight of one another, and the sound of dogs barking and cocks crowing in one state can be heard in another, yet the people of one state will grow old and die without having had any dealings with those of another.

LXXXI

Truthful words are not beautiful; beautiful words are not truthful. Good words are not persuasive; persuasive words are not good. He who knows has no wide learning; he who has wide learning does not know.
The sage does not hoard.

> Having bestowed all he has on others, he has yet more;

> Having given all he has to others, he is richer still.

The way of heaven benefits and does not harm; the way of the sage is bountiful and does not contend.